My World of Science

TRANSPARENT AND OPAQUE

Angela Royston

Heinemann

www.heinemann.co.uk/library
Visit our website to find out more information about **Heinemann Library** books.

To order:
☎ Phone 44 (0) 1865 888066
🖹 Send a fax to 44 (0) 1865 314091
💻 Visit the Heinemann Bookshop at www.heinemann.co.uk/library to browse our
catalogue and order online.

First published in Great Britain by Heinemann
Library, Halley Court, Jordan Hill, Oxford
OX2 8EJ, part of Harcourt Education.

Heinemann is a registered trademark of Harcourt
Education Ltd.

Editorial: Andrew Farrow and Dan Nunn
Design: Jo Hinton-Malivoire and
    Tinstar Design Limited (www.tinstar.co.uk)
Picture Research: Maria Joannou and Sally Smith
Production: Viv Hichens

Originated by Blenheim Colour Ltd
Printed and bound in China by
    South China Printing Company

ISBN 0 431 13739 0 (hardback)
07 06 05 04 03
10 9 8 7 6 5 4 3 2 1

ISBN 0 431 13745 5 (paperback)
08 07 06 05 04
10 9 8 7 6 5 4 3 2 1

**British Library Cataloguing
in Publication Data**
Royston, Angela
Transparent and opaque. – (My world of science)
1. Transparency – Juvenile literature
2. Opacity (Optics) – Juvenile literature
I. Title
535.3

A full catalogue record for this book is available
from the British Library.

Acknowledgements
The publishers would like to thank the following
for permission to reproduce photographs:
Eye Ubiquitous/Craig Hutchins p. **19**; Getty Images
pp. **12, 18, 22, 28**; Martin Sookias p. **15**; Network
Photographers p. **20**; Photodisc p. **5**; Ruper Horrox
p. **14**; Science Photo Library/Rudiger Lehnen p. **9**;
Trevor Clifford pp. **6, 7, 8, 10, 11, 16, 17, 21, 23,
24, 25, 26, 27, 29**; Trip pp. **4** (H. Rogers),
13 (L. Gullachsen).

Cover photograph reproduced with permission of
Trevor Clifford.

Every effort has been made to contact copyright
holders of any material reproduced in this book.
Any omissions will be rectified in subsequent
printings if notice is given to the publishers.

Contents

Any words appearing in the text in bold, **like this**,
are explained in the Glossary.

What is transparent?

You can see the **starfish** in this pool. This is because you can see through the water. The water is said to be **transparent**.

We see when light from an object enters our eyes. You can see the food inside a glass jar. Light coming from the food travels through the glass to your eyes.

What is opaque?

This girl cannot see what is inside the wooden box. The wood blocks light so the light cannot pass through it. Wood is said to be **opaque**.

These children do not want to see what each other is doing. They have put an opaque **screen** between them to block each other's view.

What is translucent?

This glass vase allows some light to pass through it. But you cannot see the stalks of the flowers clearly. The vase is **translucent**.

This water is translucent. You can see that there is a **shipwreck** in the distance. But the water is too cloudy for you to see it clearly.

Letting light through

Glass can be **transparent** or **opaque** or **translucent**. Which of these vases is opaque? Which one is the most transparent? (Answers on page 31.)

When something blocks light it makes a **shadow**. An opaque object makes a stronger shadow than a translucent object. A transparent object makes the faintest shadow.

Windows

Most windows are made of clear glass. The glass allows you to see through them to the world outside. It also stops rain and wind from blowing in.

The windows in this door are made of **translucent** glass. They allow some light in, but not enough for anyone to see through them.

Light shades

Electric light bulbs are very bright. This light shade is **translucent**. It allows some of the light through but not enough to hurt your eyes.

This light shade is **opaque**. Light cannot pass through it. The light shines only on the desk below. This stops the light annoying other people nearby.

Bottles and jars

Many bottles and jars are **transparent**. They allow you to see how much is in them. Which of these bottles is the fullest? (Answer on page 31.)

Some bottles and jars are **opaque**. You have to read the labels to know what is in them! Which two of these jars are not opaque? (Answer on page 31.)

Stained glass

Some windows are made of pieces of coloured glass. Sometimes the pieces make a picture. What picture does this window show? (Answer on page 31.)

Clear glass lets the most light through. The darkest colours of glass are the most **opaque**. Light colours of glass are **translucent**. They allow some light through.

Making coloured lights

Coloured glass is used to make some coloured lights. These light bulbs are made of glass of different colours. They decorate the street.

This torch can make red, green or white light. It has red and green coloured **screens**. When the green screen covers the bulb, it makes a green light.

Sunglasses

Sunglasses protect your eyes. They block out harmful rays from the Sun. These harmful rays can damage your eyes.

Sunglasses are **translucent**. They only allow some light to pass through them. This makes it easier for you to see in bright sunlight.

Plastic

Plastic can be **transparent** or **opaque**. The plastic covering these toy snakes allows you to see the snakes before you buy them. The plastic keeps the toys clean.

Compact disks and **games cartridges** are opaque. You cannot see through them. The compact disks are stored inside transparent plastic boxes.

Paper

Most kinds of paper are **opaque**. You cannot see through this wrapping paper to the present inside. And you cannot see through the pages of this book.

Tissue paper is made of very thin paper. Tissue paper is so thin that it is **translucent**. You can see some light shining through these paper flowers.

Cloth

Most cloth is **opaque**. Many windows have curtains or blinds that you draw at night. They stop people looking in. They also stop street lights from keeping you awake.

Some cloth is **translucent**. This bride is wearing a net **veil** over her face. She can see out, but we cannot see her face clearly.

Glossary

compact disk disk on which music is stored
games cartridge thing that computer games are stored on so that you can play them
opaque not allowing any light to pass through. You say *oh-payk*.
screen piece of thin material
shadow dark patch formed when some light is blocked
shipwreck remains of a ship that has sunk while at sea
starfish star-shaped animal often found in rock pools
translucent allowing some light to pass through, but not enough to make it see-through. You say *trans-loo-sent*.
transparent allowing light to pass through so that it is see-through. You say *trans-pa-rent*.
veil piece of cloth used to cover someone's face

Answers

page 10
The vase on the right is **opaque**. The most **transparent** vase is the one in the middle.

page 16
The fourth bottle is the fullest.

page 17
The mustard jar (on the right) and the tomato sauce jar (third from the left) are not opaque. You can see through the jars but you cannot see through the labels. The labels are opaque.

page 18
The window shows a lion.

Index